The Birth o~ ~

Written by
Dee Leone

Illustrated by
Janet Armbrust

Cover Illustrated by
Judy Hierstein

Cover Designed by
Nehmen-Kodner

All rights reserved—Printed in the U.S.A.
Copyright © 1999 Shining Star Publications
A Division of Frank Schaffer Publications, Inc.
23740 Hawthorne Blvd., Torrance, CA 90505

Dedication
For Tommy and Kathy

Notice! Pages may be reproduced for home or classroom use only, not for commercial resale. No part of this publication may be reproduced for storage in a retrieval system, or transmitted in any form or by any means—electronic, mechanical, recording, etc.—without the prior written permission of the publisher. Reproduction of these materials for an entire school or school system is strictly prohibited.

Unless otherwise indicated, the New International Version of the Bible was used in preparing the activities in this book. Scripture taken from the HOLY BIBLE, NEW INTERNATIONAL VERSION. Copyright © 1973, 1978, 1984 International Bible Society. Used by permission of Zondervan Bible Publishers.

Table of Contents

Introduction 3
Story Stickers 4–5

An Angel Visits Mary
Picture Story 6
Activity Pages 7–10
Song, Game, and Idea Page 11

Journey to Bethlehem
Picture Story 12
Activity Pages 13–16
Song, Game, and Idea Page 17

Jesus Is Born
Picture Story 18
Activity Pages 19–22
Song, Game, and Idea Page 23

A Stable Full of Animals
Picture Story 24
Activity Pages 25–28
Song, Game, and Idea Page 29

Shepherds in the Field
Picture Story 30
Activity Pages 31–34
Song, Game, and Idea Page 35

The Angels Sing
Picture Story 36
Activity Pages 37–40
Song, Game, and Idea Page 41

Wise Men From the East
Picture Story 42
Activity Pages 43–45
Song, Game, and Idea Page 46

Answer Key 47–48

© Shining Star Publications

SS48790

Introduction

Young children will have a wonderful time as they learn all about the events surrounding the birth of Jesus Christ. This book contains delightful picture stories about the birth of Jesus, activity pages to reinforce each story, and songs and ideas to supplement each of the seven units. The pages of each unit can be put together to form keepsake booklets that children will treasure for a long time.

Each unit begins with a simplified Bible story given in words and pictures. Children can participate in the reading of each story by supplying the word for each given picture (see pages 4–5 for descriptions) while the parent or teacher reads the text. Children can then use the picture clues to retell the story in their own words. Finally, the children can color the pictures.

In addition to the picture stories are exciting and stimulating activity pages to go along with each story. (An answer key is provided on pages 47–48.) They reinforce story concepts and provide practice with numbers, colors, opposites, making comparisons, and other skills. Very young children who have not yet developed small motor skills will enjoy doing many of the activities orally. Older children will be able to complete the written activities after an adult or older child reads the directions to them. It is suggested that one part of the directions at a time be read. As a child completes the activity which corresponds to a specific part of the directions, additional directions can be read.

Bible verses on the activity pages are provided as a reference. They are taken from the New International Version of the Bible. They can be read to the children or used to help explain to the children what the activities are about. Older children can memorize some of the simpler parts of the verses.

Each unit ends with an idea page filled with songs, projects, discussion topics, and more, dedicated to enriching the Bible story. This idea page can be used in the classroom or sent home.

Located on pages 4 and 5 are stickers relating to each story. Review these so that you can let the children know what or whom each picture represents. Then make copies of these for the children. The stickers can be cut out by children who have developed adequate motor skills, or an adult or older child can cut out the stickers for very young children. After reviewing the names of the sticker shapes (circle, square, rectangle, etc.), let the children color them with markers or crayons. They can then be used for a wonderful variety of activities and crafts. For example, a mixture of water and glue or mucilage can be added to the backs, and the stickers can be used for decorating stationery, for sealing envelopes, as rewards, etc. Or, they can be strung together to make Bible story necklaces or placed on small banners. Or, enlarge them for use on greeting cards, bulletin board displays, or mobiles. They can also be enlarged, mounted on heavy paper, and cut into pieces to make puzzles.

All of the pages and ideas in this book provide a wonderful way to introduce children to the birth of Jesus.

Story Stickers

These sticker pictures can be colored and cut out. Children can then use them for a wonderful variety of activities and crafts (see Introduction on page 3 for ideas).

An Angel Visits Mary—Page 6

Angel Nazareth Mary Jesus

Journey to Bethlehem—Page 12

Joseph People Mary Bethlehem Donkey

Jesus Is Born—Page 18

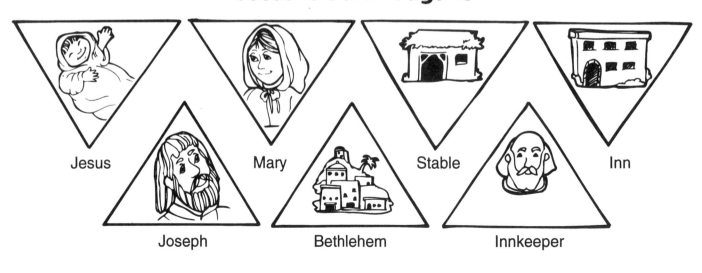

Jesus Mary Stable Inn
Joseph Bethlehem Innkeeper

Story Stickers continued

A Stable Full of Animals—Page 24

Manger   Rooster   Donkey   Cow   Dove   Stable   Jesus

Shepherds in the Field—Page 30

Jesus   Shepherds   Sheep   Manger   Angel   Bethlehem   People

The Angels Sing—Page 36

Manger   Jesus   Earth   Shepherds   Bethlehem   Angels

Wise Men From the East—Page 42

Jesus   Bethlehem   Mary   Wise Men   Camels   Gifts   Gold   Star

© Shining Star Publications

An Angel Visits Mary
(A Story Based on Luke 1:26–38)

One day, God sent the Gabriel to a town called where

a young woman named lived. The said, "Greetings. The

Lord is with you." was a little frightened. But the  said,

"Don't be afraid. God has chosen you to be the mother of His own Son. You

are to call Him ." "But can this really happen to me?"

asked the . "Yes, God can make it happen," the

answered. "I am the Lord's servant. I will do what God wants," told

the . Then, the  left her.

The Angel Greets Mary

The angel went to her and said, "Greetings, you who are highly favored! The Lord is with you." (Luke 1:28)

Find 5 things that are wrong with this picture.
Put an **X** on each one.

A Is for Angel

But the angel said to her, "Do not be afraid, Mary, you have found favor with God."
(Luke 1:30)

Circle the A's and a's that are hidden in the picture.

Trace and write the letters.

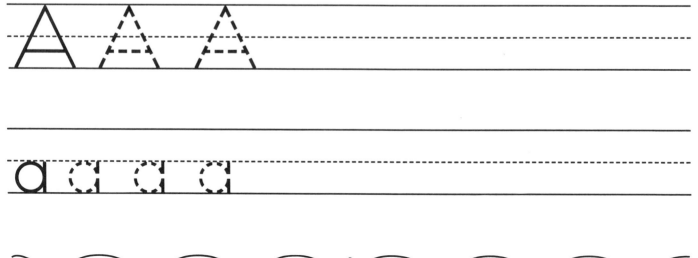

8

Mary Serves the Lord

"I am the Lord's servant," Mary answered. "May it be to me as you have said." Then the angel left her. (Luke 1:38)

Color the 2 in each row that look the same.

1   2   3   4

God Sends an Angel

... God sent the angel Gabriel to Nazareth, a town in Galilee, to a virgin ... The virgin's name was Mary. (Luke 1:26–27)

Help the angel find the way to Nazareth.

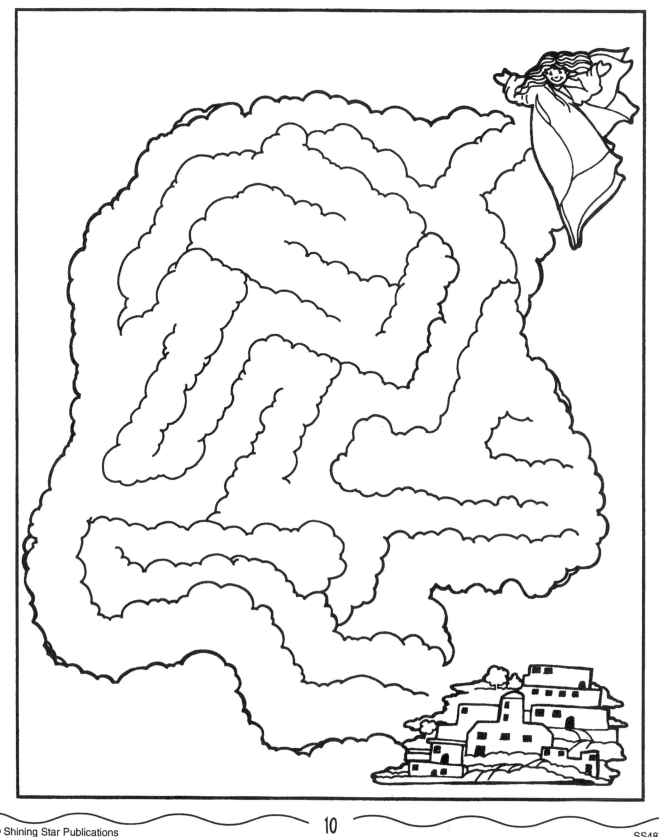

Song, Game, and Idea Page

Mary Had a Visitor
(Sing to "Mary Had a Little Lamb.")

Mary had a visitor,
Visitor, visitor.
Mary had a visitor
And Gabriel was his name.

Gabriel told Mary,
Mary, Mary,
Gabriel told Mary,
"God has chosen you."

"You will have a baby,
Baby, baby.
You will have a baby,
And Jesus will be His
   name."

Mary promised Gabriel,
Gabriel, Gabriel.
Mary promised
   Gabriel,
"I'll do the will of God."

Who's the Angel? (game)

Choose one child to go to the back of the room and cover his or her eyes. Have the rest of the children sit in a circle and ask them all to be as good as angels. Then pick one of the angels from the circle to quietly hide behind a box, desk, or door. Ask the child who was covering his or her eyes to come back near the circle. Give the child one minute to try to figure out who the missing angel is. Play several rounds so that everyone can have a turn as either the angel or the guessing child.

Things to Do

After talking about the visit the angel Gabriel made to Mary, make a special visit to a nursing home, an orphanage, etc., to sing Christmas songs to those who are there.

Tell the children that *angel* begins with *A*. Then give each child a piece of paper with a large letter *A* on it and have the children transform it into an angel.

Things to Discuss

Talk about how Mary did what God wanted her to do even though it must have been very hard. Then ask the children to talk about things they are expected to do that are not easy. Encourage them to pray to God for help.

Journey to Bethlehem
(A Story Based Partly on Luke 2:1-7)

At the time when and lived, a leader named Caesar

Augustus decided that all the  should be counted. All the

were to go to their own towns to be counted. The town and

had to go to was called . So, left for . He took

 with him. She was expecting a child. and had to

travel a long way to . Perhaps a  helped carry their

belongings. Maybe it helped to carry , too.  and

were glad when they finally arrived in . It had been a long journey.

A Long Journey

He went there to register with Mary . . . (Luke 2:5)

Color the top picture. Circle 7 things that have been added to the bottom picture.

B Is for Bethlehem

So Joseph also went up from the town of Nazareth . . . to Bethlehem the town of David . . .
(Luke 2:4)

Circle the B's and b's that are hidden in the picture.

Trace and write the letters.

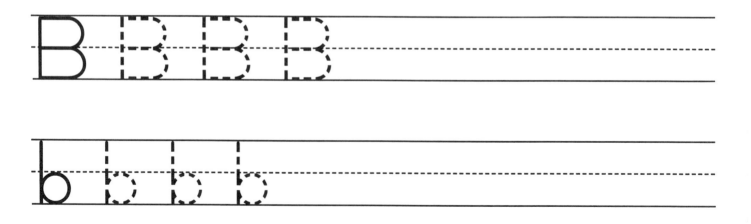

The Way to Bethlehem

And everyone went to his own town to register. (Luke 2:3)

Draw a line from each town to its matching silhouette.

A Count Is Taken

In those days Caesar Augustus issued a decree that a census should be taken of the entire Roman world. (Luke 2:1)

A census is a count. Count the number of people in each group.
Circle the number.

Song, Game, and Idea Page

The Baptism of Jesus

(Sing to "Polly Put the Kettle On.")

Joseph went to Bethlehem,
Joseph went to Bethlehem,
Joseph went to Bethlehem,
To his own hometown.

Mary went along with him, (3 times)
Upon a donkey brown.

They had to go a long, long way, (3 times)
Up the hills and down.

The baby's birth was very near, (3 times)
When they reached the town.

They tried to find an empty room, (3 times)
Not one could be found.

So, in a stable, Christ was born, (3 times)
With animals all around.

They laid Him in a manger bed, (3 times)
Set upon the ground.

Christ was born on Christmas day, (3 times)
Let the trumpets sound!

Things to Do

Let the children play "Follow the Leader to Bethlehem." Children can take turns leading the way from a starting point to a nativity scene.

Encourage children to act out in their own way what might have happened when Mary and Joseph arrived at the inn.

Things to Discuss

Ask the children to talk about differences in travel between the time when Mary and Joseph lived and now. Ask them to imagine what kind of journey it was and to think of any hardships Mary and Joseph may have faced. Then ask the children where they have traveled, what they like about traveling, and what they don't like about traveling.

Caesar, May I? (game)

This game is somewhat like the game, "Mother, May I?" The object of the game is to be first to make it from one side of the room (Nazareth) to the other side of the room (Bethlehem). In a small box, put three note cards, one numbered 1, another numbered 2, and another numbered 3. In another small box, put one note card picturing baby feet and another picturing giant feet. Children should all line up with their backs against one side of the room. The first child picks a note card from each box and then you tell him or her what to do. For example, if the child chooses a 2 and a picture of baby feet, you say, "Take two baby steps." The child must then remember to ask, "Caesar, may I?" You then respond, "Yes, you may." The child then does what he or she has been told. Baby steps are made by putting one foot right in front of the other, and giant steps are made by using the greatest strides possible. If a child forgets to ask, "Caesar, may I?," he or she must go back to the starting point.

Jesus Is Born
(A Story Based on Luke 2:6–7)

When and arrived in , they were very tired.

They went to the . "We need a place to stay," told the

. "There are no empty rooms," the said. "But our baby

will be born soon," said . "Then you may stay in the ,"

the said. So and went to the .

That night in the , had a baby boy. An no

longer mattered. Baby  had been born!

No Room in the Inn

. . . There was no room for them in the inn. (Luke 2:7)

Color the top picture. Circle 5 things that have been added to the bottom picture.

19

C Is for Christ Child

and she gave birth to her firstborn, a son . . . (Luke 2:7)

Circle the C's and c's that are hidden in the picture.

Trace and write the letters.

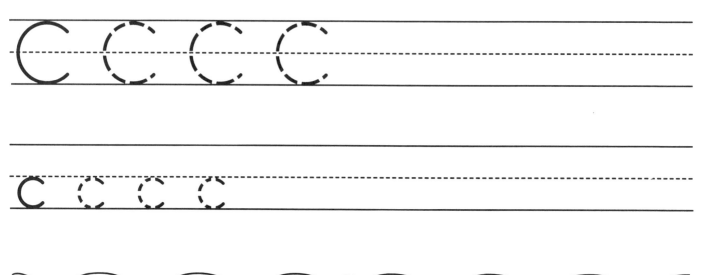

20

When Jesus Was Born

While they were there, the time came for the baby to be born. (Luke 2:6)

**Put an X on the ones that were not around when Jesus was born.
Color the ones that were around when Jesus was born.**

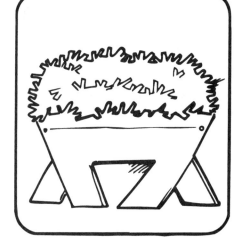  

A Manger Bed

. . . She wrapped him in cloths and placed him in a manger . . . (Luke 2:7)

Mary's husband Joseph is hidden in the picture below, and so are some birds. Find and circle Joseph and 5 birds.

Trace and write the numbers.

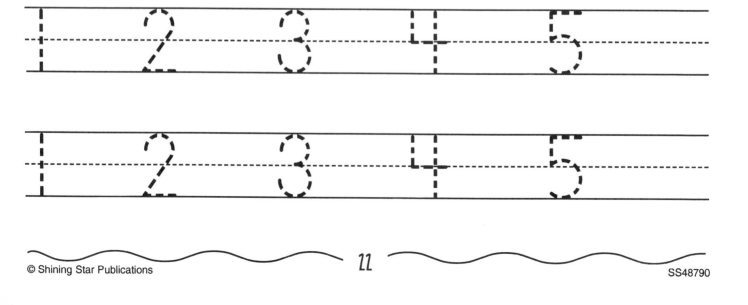

Song, Game, and Idea Page

We Wish You a Blessed Christmas

(Sing to "We Wish You a Merry Christmas.")

We wish you a blessed Christmas.
We wish you a blessed Christmas.
We wish you a blessed Christmas,
For Jesus is born.

May love and joy be with you.
May love and joy be with you.
May love and joy be with you,
For Jesus is born.

May peace spread throughout the world.
May peace spread throughout the world.
May peace spread throughout the world,
For Jesus is born.

We wish you a blessed Christmas.
We wish you a blessed Christmas.
We wish you a blessed Christmas,
For Jesus is born.

Things to Discuss

Talk about where Jesus was born. Also, discuss the special happenings surrounding the birth of Christ. Ask the children how Jesus' birth was different from their own. Ask the children what special needs a baby has and what they can do to help fill a baby's needs.

Things to Do

Let a small box serve as a manger. Every time a child does something especially well or every time a child is able to say a Christmas verse from memory, let the child add a piece of straw or yellow yarn to the manger. By Christmas, the children are sure to have done plenty of things that will lead to a manger full of soft "hay" on which baby Jesus can be laid.

Cut nativity scenes from old Christmas cards. Use a paper punch to punch holes at one-inch intervals all around the edge of each picture. These will serve as lace-up cards. Then cut several pieces of colorful yarn. Wrap a piece of masking tape at the end of each piece. Let children lace the yarn through the Christmas pictures.

In the Inn (game)

Set out a box to represent an inn. Let each child take a turn tossing ten coins, balls, beanbags, or other small objects into the inn. See how full each child can make the inn.

A Stable Full of Animals

When was born, Mary wrapped Him up gently and laid Him in a . The animals in the gathered around. When the animals saw baby , they were filled with wonder. Each had a special greeting for Him.

"Cock-a-doodle-doo," the red crowed gaily.

"Eee-haa," the gray  brayed with joy.

"Moo," the brown said in approval.

"Coo, coo," the white sang sweetly.

All the animals were happy to share their with the tiny baby.

Born in a Stable

Put an X on the 5 things that weren't around in Biblical times.

25

Counting Christmas Creatures

Count the donkeys. Circle the number.
Then use a different color to trace each donkey.

1 2 3 4 5 6 7 8 9 10

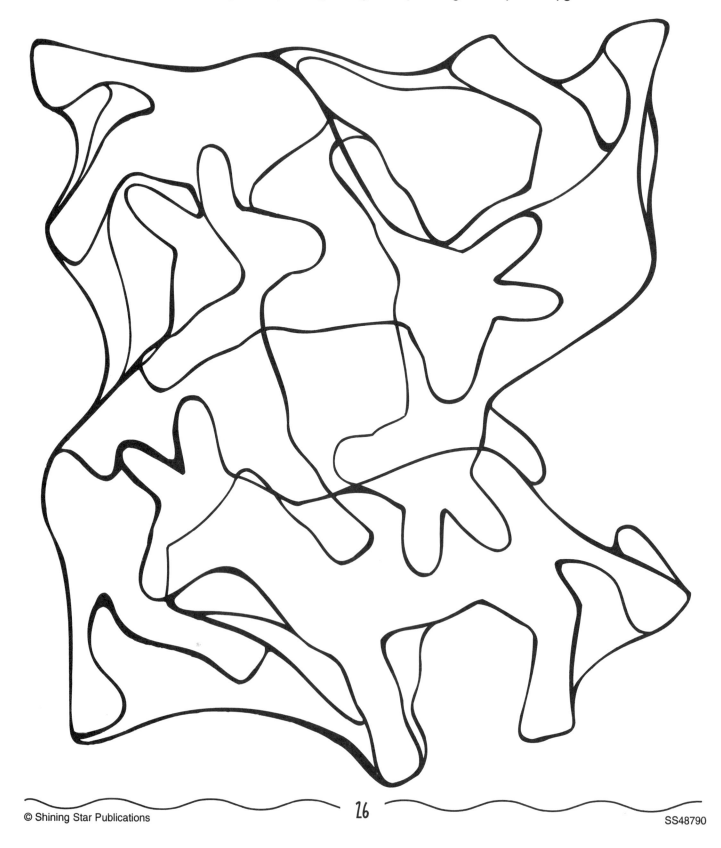

Blessed Beasts

Color the two in each group that look the same.

Six Friendly Animals

Six animals are hidden below. Find and color a cow,
a donkey, a horse, a pig, a rooster, and a dove.

Trace and write the numbers.

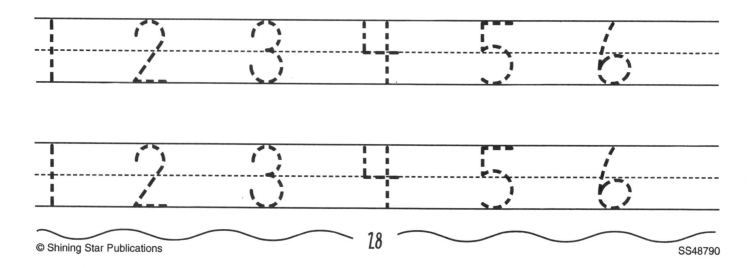

Song, Game, and Idea Page

Jesus and the Animals
(Sing to "The Ol' Gray Mare.")

Baby Jesus
Loved all the animals,
Loved all the animals,
Loved all the animals.
Baby Jesus
Loved all the animals
Many long years ago.

The old black horse, she
Gave Him a manger bed,
Gave Him a manger bed,
Gave Him a manger bed.
The old black horse, she
Gave Him a manger bed
Many long years ago.

The old brown cow, she
Gave Him some fresh clean hay, . . .

The old white sheep, she
Gave Him a blanket warm, . . .

The old white dove, she
Sang Him a lullaby, . . .

Things to Discuss
Explain to the children what a manger is. Some of them may not know it is a trough where food for animals is put. Discuss what kind of food might be found in a manger and what kinds of animals might eat from it. Then talk about ways people use animals. Encourage children to thank God for their pets or their favorite animals.

Animal Match (game)
Cut pictures of two sheep, two donkeys, two cows, two camels, etc., from magazines or coloring books and paste them on separate cards. Place the cards facedown and let children take turns turning over two cards at a time to try to find pairs.

Things to Do
Let each child pretend to be an animal. Let the other children try to guess the animal that is being acted out.

Shepherds in the Field
(A Story Based Partly on Luke 2:8–12)

When  was born, there were  in the field nearby watching over their . Suddenly, an appeared. The  were frightened to see the . "Don't be afraid," the  said. "I have good news of great joy for all . Today in a Savior has been born. You will find the baby wrapped in cloths and lying in a ." The  listened to the 's message of joy. They were filled with wonder when they heard the good news.

An Angel Appears to the Shepherds

An angel of the Lord appeared to them, and the glory of the Lord shone around them, and they were terrified. (Luke 2:9)

The shepherds were frightened when the angel appeared. Their sheep must have been frightened, too. Find and circle 5 sheep hidden in the picture.

Counting Sheep

And there were shepherds living out in the fields nearby, keeping watch over their flocks at night. (Luke 2:8)

Count the sheep in each flock. Circle the number.

Good News

But the angel said to them, "Do not be afraid. I bring you good news of great joy that will be for all the people." (Luke 2:10)

In each group, put an **X** on the one that is not the same.
Color the ones that are the same.

Taking Care of Their Sheep

And there were shepherds living out in the fields nearby, keeping watch over their flocks at night. (Luke 2:8)

Find out which sheep belong to the shepherd by following the paths. Color all the sheep that have paths that lead to the shepherd.

Song, Game, and Idea Page

Little Shepherd
(Sing to "Are You Sleeping?")

Little shepherd,
Little shepherd,
Spread the Word.
Spread the Word.
Tell of the great wonder.
Tell of the great wonder.
Christ is born.
Christ is born.

Shepherd, Shepherd, Sheep (game)

This game is played like "Duck, Duck, Goose." Children sit in a circle. One child goes around the circle lightly tapping the heads of the sitting children. As the child goes around the circle, he or she must call out "shepherd" each time he or she taps someone. At some point, the child calls out the word "sheep" instead. The "sheep" must get up quickly and try to tag the child before he or she makes it all the way around the circle and sits safely in the "sheep's" spot. The new "sheep" can become the one who recites, "Shepherd, Shepherd, Sheep," for the next round.

Things to Do

Let children practice their counting skills and number recognition skills by having them count sheep. Cut 10 large note cards into two pieces each. Use zigzags, curves, etc., to cut them apart so that no two cards are cut the same. Number half of the cards with a number from 1–10. Draw the corresponding number of sheep on each matching card. Children may count the sheep on a card and find the card with the corresponding number. This is a self-checking activity in which the correct pairs will form a simple two-piece puzzle.

Sheep Tails (game)

Hang up a drawing of a sheep without a tail. Then give each child a paper sheep tail with his or her name on the front. Put a rolled piece of masking tape on the back. Blindfold the children one at a time and let them try to tape their sheep tails as close to the right place as possible.

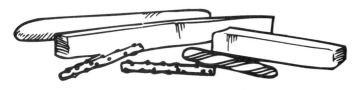

Things to Discuss

Talk about how the shepherds must have felt when the angel appeared to them. Ask the children to act out the shepherds' feelings. Encourage the children to talk about times when they've felt either frightened or surprised. Ask them to think of ways they can surprise others and make them happy.

The Angels Sing
(A Story Based Partly on Luke 2:13-20)

When  was born, an appeared to the to tell them the good news. Suddenly, more  appeared. "Glory to God in the highest," the  sang, "and peace on to all men." The listened as the joyous  sang praise to God.

When the  left, the hurried to . There, they found Mary and Joseph and baby , who was lying in a .

The were filled with joy. They spread the good news to others and praised God for everything they had seen and heard.

Heavenly Host

Suddenly a great company of the heavenly host appeared with the angel, praising God . . .
(Luke 2:13)

Color the top picture. Circle 8 things that have been added to the bottom picture.

37

The Angels Appear

Suddenly a great company of the heavenly host appeared . . . (Luke 2:13)

Can you make the angels appear?
There are 4 angels hidden below. Find and color them.

Trace and write the numbers.

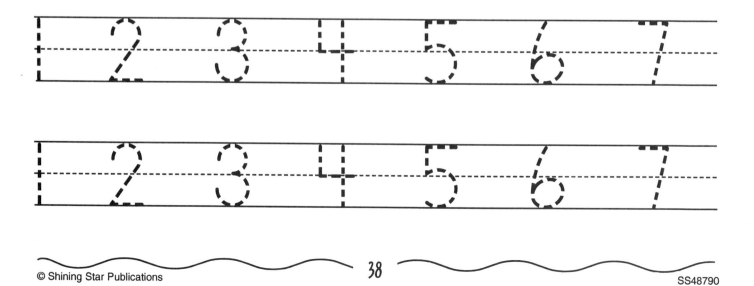

38

A Song of Praise

"Glory to God in the highest . . ." (Luke 2:14)

Draw lines to match the angels that look the same.

Peace on Earth

". . . and on earth peace to men . . ." (Luke 2:14)

Color the top picture.
Circle 5 things that are different in the bottom picture.

© Shining Star Publications

SS48790

Song, Game, and Idea Page

The Angel Band

(Sing to "The Wheels on the Bus.")

The angel's horn went
Toot toot toot, toot toot toot, toot toot toot.
The angel's horn went toot toot toot,
The day Christ was born.

The angel's drum went
Rum pum pum, rum pum pum, rum pum pum.
The angel's drum went rum pum, pum,
The day Christ was born.

The angel's bell went
Ding dong ding, ding dong ding, ding dong ding.
The angel's bell went ding dong ding,
The day Christ was born.

The angel's cymbals went
Clang clang clang, clang clang clang, clang clang clang.
The angel's cymbals went clang clang clang,
The day Christ was born.

The angel's blocks went
Clap clap clap, clap clap clap, clap clap clap.
The angel's blocks went clap clap clap,
The day Christ was born.

The angel's sticks went
Tap tap tap, tap tap tap, tap tap tap.
The angel's sticks went tap tap tap,
The day Christ was born.

(Each child may be given one of the instruments in the song to play at the appropriate time.)

Things to Discuss

Talk about the angels which appeared to the shepherds and gave praise to God. Ask children to think of ways they themselves can give praise to God.

Things to Do

Make a bulletin board or mural showing many angels. If desired, the angels may be made by the children. One way to do this is to allow each child to start with a triangular piece of wrapping paper, cloth, wallpaper, etc., to serve as the angel's gown. Children may add arms, heads, etc., and decorate the angels as desired. On the bulletin board or mural, write the words from Luke 2:14. When children memorize the verse, their names may be added to paper clouds or musical notes and placed on the board. By Christmas, you're sure to have a room full of singing angels.

Wise Men From the East
(A Story Based Partly on Matthew 2:1-12)

After  was born, came from the east. They came on with . They had seen a special in the sky. The followed the . The led them to . There, the found Jesus and His mother, . Then the gave Him the special they had brought. One of the gave . Another gave incense. Yet another gave Him myrrh.

The were full of joy! They had seen baby .

The Magi Worship Jesus

On coming to the house, they saw the child with his mother Mary, and they bowed down and worshiped him. (Matthew 2:11a)

There are 3 camels, a star, and a treasure box hidden in the picture below. Find and circle them.

Following a Star

. . . the star they had seen in the east went ahead of them until it stopped over the place where the child was. (Matthew 2:9)

Count the number in each group. Circle the number.

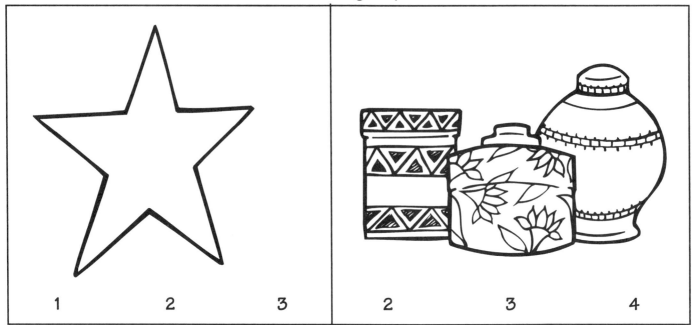

Three Gifts for the Newborn King

Then they opened their treasures and presented him with gifts of gold and of incense and of myrrh. (Matthew 2:11b)

Put an **X** on the one that is not the same.
Color the ones that are the same.

Magi From the East

After Jesus was born in Bethlehem in Judea, during the time of King Herod, Magi from the east came to Jerusalem. (Matthew 2:1)

Color the picture using the number code given.

1—red 2—green 3—orange 4—yellow 5—blue 6—brown

Song, Game, and Idea Page

 ## Must Be Wise Men

(Sing to "Must Be Santa.")

Who came to see the newborn king?
Wise men came to see the newborn king.
Who had precious gifts to bring?
Wise men had precious gifts to bring.
Gifts to bring, newborn king—
Must be wise men, must be wise men,
Must be wise men from the east.

Who came from eastern lands afar?
Wise men came from eastern lands afar.
Who knew to follow a big, bright star?
Wise men knew to follow a big, bright star.
Big, bright star, lands afar,
Gifts to bring, newborn king—
Must be wise men, must be wise men,
Must be wise men from the east.

Who found the baby sweet and mild?
Wise men found the baby sweet and mild.
Who bowed down and worshipped the child?
Wise men bowed down and worshipped the child.
Worshipped the child, sweet and mild,
Big, bright star, lands afar,
Gifts to bring, newborn king—
Must be wise men, must be wise men,
Must be wise men from the east.

(If desired, a leader or group of children can sing the questions. The rest of the children can sing the answers. Everyone can join in singing the ending to each verse. Picture clues such as the wise men worshipping the child, the baby sweet and mild, a big bright star, etc., can be used as visual aids in helping to sing the song.)

Things to Do

Cut paper towel tubes into rings that are about one inch wide. Cover each one with a piece of felt. Cut zigzag pieces off so that the resulting product looks like a crown. Give each child three of these to represent the three kings. Explain to the children, though, that the Bible does not refer to the wise men as kings, nor does it say how many wise men there were. Allow the children to decorate the crowns with glitter, sequins, beads, bric-a-brac, etc. The finished products will make wonderful napkin rings for holiday meals.

After a discussion of the star that guided the wise men to Jesus, children will enjoy decorating star-shaped cookies with icing, candy sprinkles, etc.

Things to Discuss

Discuss the gifts the wise men brought to Jesus. Ask the children what they would have brought to Jesus. Talk about the many kinds of gifts we have—love, material goods, talents, etc. Ask children what kinds of gifts they can give that don't cost money.

© Shining Star Publications

SS48790

Answer Key

Page 7

Page 8

Page 9

1 and 3, 1 and 3, 2 and 4, 2 and 4

Page 13

Page 14

Page 15

1 and 6, 2 and 4, 3 and 5

Page 16

2, 3, 5, 1

Page 19

Page 20

Page 21

Page 22

Page 25

Answer Key

Page 26

4 donkeys

Page 27

sheep 1 and 2, cows 2 and 3, donkeys 1 and 3, doves 2 and 3

Page 28

Page 31

Page 32

6, 3, 2, 7

Page 33

3, 2, 4

Page 34

1, 3, 4, 5

Page 37

Page 38

Page 39

1 and 6, 2 and 5, 3 and 4

Page 40

Page 43

Page 44

1, 3; X on 3